Grolier

DISCARD

Nature's Children

MEERKATS

Tim Harris

GROLIER

FACTS IN BRIEF

Classification of Meerkats

Class: *Mammalia* (mammals)

Order: *Carnivora* (carnivores)

Family: *Herpestidae* (mongooses). Some experts put meerkats and other *Herpestidae* in the family *Viverridae*, which also includes civets and genets.

Genus: *Suricata*

Species: *Suricata suricatta*

World distribution.   Southern Africa, from South Africa through Botswana and Namibia to Angola.

Habitat.   Dry plains, semidesert, and desert.

Distinctive physical characteristics.   Sandy-brown color with darker tail. Long, thin body with four short limbs.

Habits.   Live in packs of up to 40 animals. Sleep in burrows.

Diet.   Mostly insects, such as beetles and ants, and also scorpions. Also lizards, mice, and amphibians. Sometimes they eat plants or their roots.

© 2004 The Brown Reference Group plc
Printed and bound in U.S.A.
Edited by John Farndon and Angela Koo

Published by:

An imprint of Scholastic Library Publishing
Old Sherman Turnpike, Danbury,
Connecticut 06816

Library of Congress Cataloging-in-Publication Data

Harris, Tim.
     Meerkats / Tim Harris. -- *Danbury, CT: Grolier, 2004.*
     48 p.: col. ill.; p. cm. — (Nature's children)
     Includes index.
     Summary: Describes the physical characteristics, habits, and natural environment of meerkats.
     ISBN 0–7172–5957–9 (set)   ISBN 0–7172–5969–2
     1. Meerkat—Juvenile literature. [1. Meerkat.] I. Title. II. Series.

QL737.C235H37 2004
599.74'2—dc21

2003049171

599.74
HAR

Contents

With their beady black eyes and playful behavior the meerkats of the dry plains of southern Africa are some of the cutest animals you are ever likely to see. They often stand upright on their back legs, propped up by their tail. Their front legs dangle down in front of them. Often meerkats stand side by side, turning their head this way and that to see what is happening around them.

The remarkable thing about meerkats is the way gangs of them work together. Every member of the group plays his or her part in helping the whole community. They hunt together, sleep together, and even take turns caring for their children. If one meerkat spots danger, it gives a warning bark so all the others can flee to their burrows.

Mother meerkats are very protective of their babies and leave them with a babysitter if they have to go out.

Desert Survivors

The name "meerkat" comes from a South African Dutch (Afrikaans) word meaning "lake cat." But meerkats are not cats, just cat-sized, and don't live near lakes. In fact, they live in dry regions of southern Africa in Botswana, Namibia, South Africa, and Angola. They even live in the very heart of the Kalahari and Namib Deserts. In places there it rains only twice a year. The summer sun may heat the desert sand to a scorching 160°F (71°C).

Still, meerkats are well adapted to these extreme conditions. They like the soft sand, too, because it is easy to dig in. They don't like their sand too soft, though, because their burrows would cave in.

There are three different kinds of meerkat, and their color varies to match the sand they live in. There are orange-colored meerkats living on the yellow sands of South Africa. Silvery white meerkats live on the white sands of the Namib and Kalahari Deserts. In Angola the meerkats tend to be tan colored.

*Meerkats live in very warm, dry, often desertlike
places where the sandy soil makes good burrows.*

Relations

Meerkats belong to a family of mammals called mongooses. Mongooses are small creatures with long tails that live in warm places in Africa and Asia. With their short legs and slender bodies they look a little like weasels—and are perfectly built for scurrying down burrows after prey such as insects and mice. They are such good snake killers it was once thought they were immune to snake poison. They are not; they are just very quick.

The mongooses are closely related to a group of similar creatures called viverrids, including civets and genets. Civets and genets look a little like stubby-legged cats with long, pointed snouts and bushy tails. While mongooses hunt by day, civets and genets come out only at night. Some experts group civets, genets, and mongooses together in one big family called the Viverridae (said vi-VEH-rid-eye).

Opposite page: *The yellow mongoose is the meerkat's closest relative. It lives in many of the same places, such as the Kalahari Desert in southern Africa.*

9

Made for the Desert

Opposite page:
Meerkats look like they're wearing sunglasses. In a way they are; they have a dark ring around their eyes that keeps them from getting dazzled by the desert sun.

An adult meerkat's body is around 12 inches (30 centimeters) long. That is about the length of a house cat. Its tail adds another 7 inches (18 centimeters). A meerkat's legs are short, and its tail is strong enough to act as a third "leg" or brace when it is standing upright.

A meerkat's body perfectly suits its lifestyle. Being long and thin, it loses heat quickly. That is important for an animal that lives in very hot places.

Meerkats are covered by a thin coat of fur —enough to keep them warm at night, but not too thick that they overheat during the day. The fur is sandy brown with faint black stripes. These colors help camouflage (hide) meerkats in the dusty places where they live.

Meerkats have a long snout for poking around in the earth for food. They also have four sharp teeth, called canines, at the front of their mouth and scissor-shaped teeth (molars) behind. The canines grasp prey, while the molars grind it into easy-to-swallow chunks.

A meerkat gang does everything together—like this gang on sentry duty, watching out for trouble.

Gang Rule

Meerkat society is very well organized. The animals live in groups called gangs. They cooperate for the benefit of all. The smallest gangs have only four or five members, but sometimes up to 40 meerkats gang up together. Meerkat gangs often have aunts and uncles as well as moms, dads, and babies. The babies are called pups or kits.

Every animal in the gang benefits from membership in this special club. The warning calls of one meerkat alert all the others to danger. If an enemy attacks one member, all the others rush to its aid. If a mom is struggling to bring up her pups, all the other gang members help, either by feeding them or taking a turn at babysitting. Not surprisingly, bigger gangs have more success chasing off enemies and raising their young. That is because there are more animals to dig for food, watch for danger, and—should the need arise—fight.

A Meerkat's Day

Opposite page:
Meerkats usually emerge from their burrows very early in the morning before the sun gets too hot to bear.

Soon after sunrise the air outside the meerkats' burrow starts to warm up. One by one the sleepy animals emerge from their burrow to stand or lie in the sunshine. They are careful when they come out, just in case there is a snake or jackal waiting to attack. Then all those in the day's hunting party scamper away from the burrow and begin the search for food. Adults and young alike join in. One meerkat stands alert on a raised area of ground or in a bush, watching for danger. Back at the burrow a few pups too young to go looking for food are cared for by an older brother or sister.

As the sun rises higher in the sky, it gets too hot for hunting to go on. All the meerkats seek the shade of their burrow or another animal's hole to pass the hottest hours of the day. They come out again in the late afternoon. Meerkats are active only during the day. As the sun sets, they go back to their burrow, huddle up in a furry ball, and go to sleep.

Digging for a Meal

Meerkats are great diggers. They dig burrows for homes, and they dig holes in search of food. A meerkat can dig out its own body weight in sand in just a few seconds. In a single morning one meerkat may dig out several hundred holes. Dry desert sand is soft and loose, but that is still amazing digging.

What makes meerkats so good at excavating? They dig mostly with the claws on their front feet. A digging meerkat can scratch at the ground several hundred times a minute. Sometimes meerkats dig so deep that they disappear under the surface. Like other mammals, meerkats can shut their eyes to protect them. They also have a special white layer under their eyes. This layer acts like a windshield wiper when they blink. And they can do something even more clever: They can shut their ears! The outer part of their ears is covered in ridges and flaps that can join together and keep sand from getting in.

Underground Shelters

During the day meerkats are busy above ground, alert to every danger. But at night they retreat to the safety of their burrows. They also scurry into their burrows when danger threatens, or when it simply gets too hot outside. Meerkats often move into burrows dug by other small mammals. The meerkats' burrow may have 15 different entrances. So if a deadly snake enters one way, the occupants can make their escape through another hole.

Meerkats make a separate den where the animals can sleep at night and a room where pups can be cared for. They lay dead grass on the floor of the pups' den. There may be two or three levels of tunnels in a burrow network, with the deepest down to 6 feet (2 meters) below the surface. Each gang of meerkats has a home patch called a territory. A gang with a large territory may have four or five burrows, so the animals can move from one area to another in search of food.

Hungry Hunters

Meerkats eat many kinds of food. Popular snacks include insects (such as termites), worms, snails, and scorpions, as well as roots and bulbs. Sometimes they eat larger animals, such as lizards and mice. Meerkats hardly ever drink water; they get the liquid their bodies need from juicy bugs and grubs.

Most of the small creatures that meerkats eat live underground. So to find them, the meerkat has to sniff them out with its sensitive nose, then dig into the ground with its claws.

Meerkats love scorpions despite the sting in their tail. They quickly nip off the sting with their teeth and spit it out before the scorpion can strike. Sometimes meerkats drag poisonous insects such as millipedes across the sand to wear out the poison.

When meerkats hunt larger animals, they often hunt in groups. Several meerkats dig together to root out a mouse hidden in the sand. That way they get to their food quicker. Once caught, the food is shared.

With their stinging tails scorpions can be a
dangerous meal, but meerkats love them.

Territory Defenders

Each gang of meerkats has its own patch of land, or territory. A territory may be large or small. The biggest may be 9 square miles (15 square kilometers). The lead (dominant) male meerkat in a gang smears scent around the territory to warn off members of other gangs. People cannot smell the scent, but meerkats have an excellent sense of smell. They can even check which animals are members of their gang by sniffing them. If a meerkat from one gang's patch strays into another's, there may be trouble.

A meerkat territory has to provide a gang with enough food. But if lots of pups are born, and the gang gets too big—or if food is scarce—they may try to steal some territory from a neighboring gang. They may even move in on the neighbors' burrows. The weaker gang has to move away.

Opposite page: *If a meerkat strays into another meerkat gang's patch, there can be a nasty fight.*

Sentries on Duty

Meerkats spend much of the day with their heads down, digging for food. While they are digging for food, they can't keep watch for enemies like eagles, snakes, and jackals. Their burrows can also be invaded by unwanted visitors.

Meerkats have a solution to this problem. At least one member of every gang acts as a sentry, watching alertly for a snake slithering across the sand or an eagle flying overhead. To get a better all-round view, the lookout usually stands upright on a mound of earth. Sometimes it may even climb a bush or tree to get a better view. This can create problems though. While they are good at climbing, meerkats are not so good at getting down again. As long as the coast is clear, the sentry gives out a gentle stream of mellow calls. But when an enemy is sighted, the sentry makes a beeping noise. As the enemy gets closer, the sentry gives a different call depending on the danger—so the others know just what to do.

To get the best possible view of danger, meerkats on sentry duty stand upright on their back legs.

Danger from the Skies

Out in the desert there is very little cover. So meerkats are in real danger from big, fierce hunting birds such as martial eagles and goshawks. The meerkats have sharp eyes, so they can spot danger from afar. But birds can be hard to see against the dazzling desert sky. Luckily, meerkats have a dark ring round their eyes that acts like sunglasses. So the sentry can see a bird swooping right out of the sun.

If the meerkat sentry spies an eagle or a hawk, it lets out a long howl. At once the other meerkats stand still to spot the danger—then make a bolt for their burrow. If they can't reach the burrow in time, they dash for shelter under a thornbush. And if that fails, they simply lie down, hoping not to be seen. When the danger is over, the sentry makes a low peeping call. Some people call it the "watchman's song."

Opposite page: *This is a sight a meerkat does not want to see—a martial eagle. Martial eagles are the meerkats' most fearsome enemy.*

Danger on the Ground

Hunting birds are not the meerkat's only enemies. On the ground there are always prowling jackals and wildcats to fear. When a meerkat sentry spots a jackal, it bobs its head up and down, trying to judge how near it is. As the jackal moves in, the sentry gives a low, gruff double bark.

But the meerkats don't always run. If a jackal gets too close to the pups, the meerkats mob together to drive it off. They fluff up their fur to make themselves look bigger and hiss fiercely. Usually the jackal slinks away.

Sometimes a snake tries to get into the meerkats' burrow. Again, the gang mobs together to drive it away. Usually they are quick enough to escape the snake's poisonous bite. Sometimes, though, even the mob's best efforts fail, and the snake carries off a pup.

A jackal on the prowl spells danger for meerkats.
But if they get together, they can often drive it off.

A Loyal Band

Meerkats spend a lot of their time combing each other's fur. This is called grooming, and it is important for two reasons. It keeps the animals' fur clean and free of bugs. It also helps build bonds of friendship between the different gang members. Loyalty to the gang is very strong. If one gang member moves away from the others, the rest follow so that it is not left alone.

The gang's strong community spirit helps it survive through hard times. If any member is in trouble, the other meerkats help it, even if it is not a close relative. Sons, daughters, mothers, fathers, aunts, uncles, cousins, and even meerkats that have been adopted from other gangs are treated equally.

Meerkats are a very friendly bunch and stick close together. They need to in order to survive in the desert.

Breeding

Opposite page: *When a male and female meerkat want to get together, they often wrestle like this. The fight can get quite wild before they settle down at last to mate.*

Meerkats can mate and produce young once they are around a year old. When a female is ready to mate, she picks a play fight with the male. This starts an exciting courtship dance. The pair wrestle, jump, and snap at each other. Sometimes they may even bite. The female jumps up and down, crouches, sticks her tail in the air, and makes purring noises before allowing the male to mate with her.

A male meerkat is free to mate with any grown-up female in his gang. However, it is usually only the oldest and most experienced male and female that mate. These meerkats are called the dominant male and female. Around eight out of every ten offspring are born to the dominant female. She may have three litters a year, so in a typical lifetime of around eight years she may give birth to several dozen babies.

Meerkat pups are quite helpless when they're small and need constant looking after.

Caring for the Babies

A female meerkat is pregnant for around
10 weeks before giving birth to her babies,
which are called pups. She may have just one
baby in her litter, but three or four are more
common. All the time she is pregnant, the
mom goes out hunting with the other meerkats.
She gives birth in a special part of the burrow
called a nursery den.

At first, the babies are quite helpless. They
have no fur; they cannot see or hear and can
hardly move. If the mother meerkat has to
move them, she lifts them by the scruff of the
neck the way a cat lifts her kittens. The pups
feed on their mom's milk. Milk feeding is
called suckling. While only some adults
breed, the others devote much of their lives to
helping the breeding animals raise their young.
Sometimes other females produce milk at the
same time to help the babies grow quickly.

Babysitters

If the mother meerkat did not leave her babies every day to search for food, her milk supply would dry up. Then the babies would starve to death. But if she left the pups alone, they would be in great danger. A snake might slither into the burrow and eat them. Meerkats have a way around this problem. While mom is away, other meerkats take turns babysitting the babies, keeping them warm and protected from their enemies. Mom returns in the evening, and the pups can suckle from her again.

A day's babysitting duty can be very tiring work. A babysitter can lose 2 percent of its body weight. Helping others raise their young is called cooperative breeding behavior. It is unusual in mammals. Mole rats, marmosets, and wild dogs also help each other, but not as much as meerkats do.

This meerkat has been left to look after the babies while their mother is off searching for food.

Even after careful lessons from mom, tackling a scorpion is a tricky business for meerkat pups.

Leaving the Burrow

When they are three or four weeks old,
the youngsters are strong enough to leave
the burrow. They already are able to stand on
their back legs, just like their parents and older
brothers and sisters. The pups keep in contact
with each other and with the grownups by
making squeaky calls.

When the pups are a little bigger, the
grownups feed them tiny bits of food, but
they continue suckling. They stay close to an
adult, constantly begging for food. The older
meerkats provide a constant feeding service for
the babies until they are old enough to fend for
themselves. Even when the young meerkats
can find their own food, an adult stays close,
teaching them how to catch different types of
food—and what to avoid.

Growing Up

Opposite page:
A mother meerkat keeps a watchful eye over a pair of pups playfully wrestling—just in case the fight gets a little too rough.

The pups must be able to feed themselves by the time they are three or four months old. If they can't, they will probably starve. Even at this age pups squabble and fight with each other. This play fighting can look very rough at times, but it helps the young meerkats grow strong and learn to look after themselves.

Sometimes young meerkats fight their older brothers and sisters and the grownups, too. However, they cannot compete on equal terms until they are about 18 months old. When the sun's heat becomes too hot to bear, the pups may bury each other in the sand. That helps keep them cool—and it is also great fun!

Summer Heat

On the dry plains of southern Africa there is quite a difference between summer and winter. Summer is very hot, and temperatures can soar to a scorching 115°F (46°C). Searching for food in this kind of heat is tiring work. So meerkats get up very early in summer to look for food. Then as the day heats up, they retreat to a nice, shady spot to rest. Pups go in first, but even the hardiest adults get out of the sun in the afternoon—perhaps in the burrow or under the roots of an old tree.

Later in the afternoon, as the sun cools, the meerkats come out to feed again. Fortunately, summer is the rainy season, too. The grasses grow tall and lush, and there is food in abundance. So although the meerkats are out foraging only a few hours a day, they are never hungry. Indeed, they are so well fed that you can often see their bellies sticking out.

Opposite page: *When the summer sun gets too hot in the middle of the day, meerkats do the only sensible thing—chill out in the shade.*

Hard Times

Winter is the hardest time for meerkats. From May to September days stay warm, but at night temperatures can plunge to well below freezing. At night the meerkats huddle together in a furry ball in their burrow to keep warm. During the day they often lie with their stomachs exposed to the sun. They have a little dark patch on their bellies that acts as a solar panel and helps warm them up.

Winter is also the dry season, and food is very scarce. The meerkats get up late because it is too cold first thing. But once they are out, they are busy all day without rest, desperately seeking scraps of food. In summer they feast on lizards and scorpions. In winter they often have to make do with ant eggs and millipedes. By about 4:30 p.m. it's getting too cold to go on hunting, and so the meerkats go back to their burrows again.

Starting Out

When some people wanted to find out more about how meerkats live their lives, they thought it would be a good idea to follow a large meerkat gang. One gang member was just six months old. The people called the young male Juma. Not long afterward disaster struck this band of meerkats—the rains failed, and they were forced to move away. Many were killed by predators.

Juma was left with just his three young sisters. Life was very hard for them. The four young meerkats stayed together for a year before Juma went missing. Had he, too, been killed? Eventually Juma was found in a different territory with two adult females and another male. Juma and one of the females mated, and the size of his new group grew to 8, then 14, then 20. What a success story! He was last seen when he was 8 years old—a good age for a meerkat.

Words to Know

Camouflage Coloring that makes meerkats look like their surroundings.

Canine teeth Any of the four sharp teeth that are found on the front of the jaws.

Dominant male A strong male in any group of animals that is boss over all the others in the group. He may be partnered by a dominant female.

Excavate To dig.

Gang A close-knit group of meerkats that live together.

Groom To clean or brush, especially hair or fur.

Mammal Any warm-blooded animal that gives birth to live young and produces milk to feed them.

Mate To come together to produce young. Either member of an animal pair is also the other animal's mate.

Mob When meerkats work together to drive off an intruder.

Molars Broad, flat teeth at the back of a meerkat's mouth. Molars grind food.

Suckle To feed babies with milk from the mother's body.

Savanna A hot, grassy plain with little rainfall and few trees.

Species A particular type of animal.

Territory An area of land that a meerkat gang lives in.

INDEX

Cover Photo: Bruce Coleman: Alain Compost

Photo credits: Ardea: Clem Haagner 26, 33, Ingrid Van den Berg 11; NHPA: Mark Bowler 4, 34, Nigel J. Dennis 7, 8, 21, 30, 41, 45, Andy Rouse 22, Anne & Steve Toon 29; Oxford Scientific Films: Tim Jackson 37, David Macdonald 12, 15, 38, 42; Still Pictures: Nigel J. Dennis 18/19.